Mentoring

Finding Personal Mentors
Mentoring Others

Self-discovery Workbook

LEADER | **Breakthru**

LEADERSHIP DEVELOPMENT
Workbooks

Each of our lives has purpose when seen in light of God and his purposes. God has created each of us to do good deeds which he authored into our lives, before time began (Ephesians 2:10).

The question is not whether God is at work IN OUR LIVES, but rather the discovery of his shaping work. This workbook series is designed to help you discover God forming our your life and how you can best join that work in the days ahead.

Perspective	Focus	Mentoring
PERSONAL TIME-LINE	**PERSONAL MISSION**	**PERSONAL MENTORS**

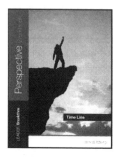

The **Mentoring** Workbook

MENTORING is one of three steps that can help lead to greater clarity and focus in your life for Christ. Each step and workbook is designed to be self-discovery and bring new clarity and focus.

MENTORING will help you better understand the concept of mentoring, and provides you a step-by-step process to identifying the mentors you need, and how to find them. It also is a great resource you can use as you teach others about mentoring.

The MENTORING PODCAST is an audio resource that helps to walk you through each step of the process of finding mentors and is the companion resource with this workbook. It can be obtained at the Leader Breakthru website:www.leaderbreakthru.com/lbu.mentoring.

*All three steps of this leadership development series have been woven together into a powerful personal discovery process called... **Focused Living.***

Focused Living is available in a variety of forms:

Focused Living On-Line (walk through an video, on-line process through each step of the process)

Focused Living Small Group (walk through the process with your group utilizing the on-line process and group notes)

Focused Living Retreat (walk through the process in a powerful large group setting or retreat setting with facilitator notes and resources.

Mentoring

Believers who finish well recognize mentoring as a priority.

Mentoring links people to the resources of others, empowering them for greater personal growth and ministry effectiveness. Mentoring is a relational experience in which one person empowers another by sharing God-given resources.

Some of the Myths of Mentoring

Some commonly held misconceptions about mentors and mentoring include:

"I used to think that a person has one mentor for life. I now realize that this is unrealistic, and even unfair, to expect one person to empower me in all the areas of my life."

"I used to think that mentors had to be older, but effective mentors can be younger if the resources they possess matches what others need."

"I used to think that I had little to offer someone else by way of mentoring or resources. I have now discovered that sometimes just believing and supporting another servant unleashes tremendous help and empowerment."

"I used to feel I could make it on my own. But in reality, I would have given up several times if it had not been for the insight and help of my mentors."

Mentoring is a self-discovery workbook that will help you better understand the concept of mentoring, and learn how to mentor others. You can learn more about mentoring by reading *Connecting* by Paul Stanley and J. Robert Clinton (NavPress: 1992),

The Four Steps of Mentoring

Step 1— Defining
What is mentoring? What does a mentor look like?
This step assists in defining mentoring and recognizing that mentoring has occurred throughout all of life.

Step 2—Assessing
What type of Mentoring do I need?
Next you will determine your mentoring goals, reviewing the nine types of mentoring and clarify your mentoring needs.

Step 3—Initiating
How do you find a mentor? And how does one initiate the mentoring relationship? Creating a mentoring constellation and understanding the ten commandments of mentoring will assist your search for mentors.

Step 4—Empowering
How do I become a mentor for others? What are the key skills involved in mentoring? Understanding the five circles of mentoring and how to introduce others to mentors helps to free you to mentor others.

Finishing Well

The Bigger Picture

The heart cry of every genuine believer is to stand at the end and hear Christ say, "well done thou good and faithful servant." It is the reason behind seeking to live a focused life. A simple definition of finishing well: *To be more passionate and committed to Christ at the end of one's life than in the beginning.*

Mentoring assists your journey toward living a focused life that pleases God, and finishes well. Before you begin *Mentoring,* take a moment to evaluate your current behavior in light of five habits that help believers to finish well.

There are FIVE HABITS that help to enhance a believers capacity to finish well. They are one result of the research of Dr. J. Robert Clinton, Professor of Leadership at Fuller Seminary in Pasadena, California. Dr. Clinton has studied over 1200 biblical, historical and contemporary servants of God. Take the Five Habits Checklist below.

1. *Effective believers maintain a learning posture throughout their entire lives.*
   They never stop learning. Whether informally (reading, personal growth, projects, personal research), non-formally (workshops, seminars, conferences) or sometimes through formal training (continuing education, degree programs).

2. **Effective believers recognize mentoring as a priority.**
   They are committed to being mentored and mentoring others God brings their way.
   This habit is the focus on this workbook and exercise.

3. *Effective believers have a dynamic statement of personal calling.*
   They allow God to continually shape their unique and ultimate contribution. A believer's calling typically emerges in late 30's and the ability to articulate in the 40's and 50's.

4. *Effective believers experience repeated times of renewal.*
   Effective, godly servants develop intimacy with God which, in turn, overflows into all of their life and ministry.

5. *Effective believers increasingly perceive their life in terms of a big-picture, lifetime perspective.* They manifest a growing awareness of their sense of destiny.

The FIVE HABITS Checklist

INSTRUCTIONS: Read each statement on pp. 5-7, and check the number on the continuum that most accurately describes you. Check "0" if the statement on the left represents you; check "5" if you feel you are described better by the statement on the right. Numbers "1" through "4" reflect various positions between the two extremes.

1. I am often frustrated by the demands of the ministry and my lack of personal growth.

|—|—|—|—|☒—|
0　1　2　3　4　5

I am able to handle the daily pressures of the ministry and still find times for reflection and growth.

Five Habits Checklist—Section One

1. I have a desire to do some personal growth projects, but I seldom have the time or discipline necessary to do so.

|—|—|—|—|—|
0   1   2   3   4   5

I view my personal development as a lifelong learning process and am regularly involved in study projects.

2. I hear of various workshops and seminars that others find helpful, but I seldom attend.

|—|—|—|—|—|
0   1   2   3   4   5

I regularly attend workshops and seminars that help enhance my personal growth and development as a leader.

3. I am simply too busy or have little desire for continuing formal education.

|—|—|—|—|—|
0   1   2   3   4   5

I enjoy my continuing education classes and am currently enrolled in an education program.

4. I do some things for myself, but I don't feel fulfilled or that I am growing as a person or leader.

|—|—|—|—|—|
0   1   2   3   4   5

I work to develop the "whole" person and set improvement goals for wide areas of personal growth development.

Section One Total [   ]

Five Habits Checklist—Section Two

1. I feel overwhelmed by the needs of the ministry and seldom, if ever, spend time developing new leaders.

|—|—|—|—|—|
0   1   2   3   4   5

I am always in the process of developing a pool of new leaders to release into ministry.

2. It is often hard for me to imagine that I have something to offer in a mentoring relationship to others.

|—|—|—|—|—|
0   1   2   3   4   5

I generally have a good estimation of the strengths and abilities I can offer to other leaders.

3. I feel "alone" in the ministry and feel there are few who are helping me grow.

|—|—|—|—|—|
0   1   2   3   4   5

I deeply value others and have a regular series of relationships that help me grow and develop.

4. I don't know what my actual developmental needs are or how a mentor could help.

|—|—|—|—|—|
0   1   2   3   4   5

I view my development as a high priority and have obtained mentors to help ensure my ongoing growth.

Section Two Total [   ]

Five Habits Checklist—Section Three

1. I often feel frustrated, wondering if I am doing what God really intends for me.

|—|—|—|—|—|
0   1   2   3   4   5

I feel the things I do every day are meaningful and part of my biblical purpose and reason for existence.

2. I sometimes get glimpses of what I should do with my life, but somehow these visionary moments get lost in busy activity.

|—|—|—|—|—|
0   1   2   3   4   5

I have thought deeply about why I exist as a person and have clarified my personal vision and what God is calling me to accomplish.

3. I often work based upon the need of the moment as opposed to a clear philosophy of ministry.

|—|—|—|—|—|
0   1   2   3   4   5

I am able to decide what is important for me to do, basing my decisions upon a clear ministry philosophy.

4. I am easily frustrated by changes in the direction of ministry or in my life situation.

|—|—|—|—|—|
0   1   2   3   4   5

I feel like I have a clear direction, but I allow God to teach me new things and alter how I should minister.

Section Three Total [   ]

Five Habits Checklist—Section Four

1. I nearly always feel "buried," having more to do than I can handle. Getting away for me seems impossible.

|—|—|—|—|—|
0   1   2   3   4   5

I regularly schedule times away for personal retreat and reflection.

2. I feel that "personal" time is selfish, especially when I am called to help minister to others.

|—|—|—|—|—|
0   1   2   3   4   5

I feel an investment in my personal walk with Christ will cause me to experience deeper intimacy with Christ and greater effectiveness.

3. If someone were to ask me how long has it been since I have felt the presence of God, I'd have to respond, "Quite some time."

|—|—|—|—|—|
0   1   2   3   4   5

I regularly experience times of renewal and freshness in my walk and intimacy with Christ.

4. Although I know the spiritual disciplines are important to real growth, I seldom have time to focus on them.

|—|—|—|—|—|
0   1   2   3   4   5

My walk with Christ is greatly enhanced through regular usage of a variety of spiritual disciplines.

Section Four Total [   ]

1. I have trouble rising above the current circumstances to get a big-picture perspective on my life.

|—|—|—|—|—|
0   1   2   3   4   5

I earnestly try to understand my current circumstance in light of what God has been doing over my lifetime.

2. I realize that God is shaping my life, but I seldom am able to understand how He is at work in my life.

|—|—|—|—|—|
0   1   2   3   4   5

I feel that the things that happen to me every day are part of God's development of my life, and I can recognize patterns of His work.

3. I have trouble trying to keep track of the many areas of my life: home, office, etc.

|—|—|—|—|—|
0   1   2   3   4   5

I feel a sense of order in my life because I am able to regularly gain perspective on my life.

4. I hear other leaders talk about their calling and vision, but I rarely feel I have a sense of destiny.

|—|—|—|—|—|
0   1   2   3   4   5

In my times with Christ, I continue to sense a unique, personal destiny that He has for my life.

Section Five Total [   ]

Summary

Go back and total your score in each section. Record your totals in the boxes Review your scores. Where are you strong? Weak? Look at your scores in relationship to each other.

- Habit #1 (lifelong learning) and Habit #4 (repeated times of renewal) are attitudes that a believer must commit to maintain if they are to finish well.
- Habit #5 (perspective), Habit #3 (personal calling) and **Habit #2 (mentoring)** are the three steps that comprise the *Focused Living* process.

1. Maintains a learning posture throughout life.   Section One Total [   ]

2. Commitment to being mentored and mentoring.   Section Two Total [   ]

3. Dynamic personal mission and calling.   Section Three Total [   ]

4. Repeated times of personal renewal.   Section Four Total [   ]

5. Lifetime, big-picture perspective   Section Five Total [   ]

This workbook, **Mentoring** focuses on the second habit.
The **Focused Living** process is designed to help you intentionalize the five habits into your life.

Mentoring
Defining
Mentoring

STEP 1

Understanding Mentoring

There are all types of mentoring relationships.

The relationship between mentor and mentoree may be formal or informal, scheduled or sporadic. The exchange of resources can take place over a long time or just once. Mentoring can also occur face-to-face or may happen over a great distance.

Mentors link mentorees to important resources, from financial resources to opportunities for ministry.

Mentors empower mentorees with encouragement and timely advice garnered through life.

Step one in the finding of mentors is the introduction to the paradigm of mentoring and reviewing times when mentoring has already occurred in your life, some times unaware.

You will need ... Workbook and pen.

Time required ... Approximately 1 hour.

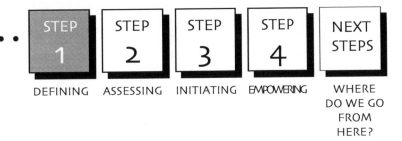

STEP 1	STEP 2	STEP 3	STEP 4	NEXT STEPS
DEFINING	ASSESSING	INITIATING	EMPOWERING	WHERE DO WE GO FROM HERE?

Defining
In Search of Mentors

Rod's Story

From the time I committed my life to Jesus Christ at the age of fifteen, there had never been a person who had taken an interest in me to the point where, over an extended period of time, he wanted to assist me in my growth as a Christian. I can never remember another person willing to disciple me.

When this fact dawned on me a few years ago, feelings of hurt and anger arose within me. I concluded that no one ever had the desire to take the initiative, perhaps because they never saw the potential in me. Consequently, I was a late starter in my Christian growth and only began to make up time as I accepted personal responsibility for my growth. I set annual goals and sought the assistance of more gifted and mature people to help me achieve these goals. By beginning to see myself as God saw me, I now had motivation to become that which God saw in me.

To some degree my feelings of hurt and anger were lessened when my surveys of Christian groups revealed that approximately two out of ten people were personally discipled in some form. This is a painful fact, and the church in my generation has suffered from this omission.

Terry's Story

I had the privilege of godly discipleship. A faithful believer and godly parents imparted to me the basics of the Christian walk. They showed me how to study God's word; how to spend daily time with God in prayer; the values of fellowship; and how to share my faith. I am eternally thankful.

But since those early days, I have struggled with a sense of lacking in the necessary skills that I need to be more effective in ministry. Upon entering full-time Christian work, I discovered that denominational structures were often ill-equipped to offer me help or resources. Seminars and books often told me what to do, but few were available to provide the "how-to" help I needed.

As I cried out to God for help I realized that I must be the one to take the initiative for my own growth. Either I could stay in a state of confusion and become more disillusioned, or I could seek out godly help.

I was challenged by a friend to clarify my personal goals. He showed me that there could be many mentors for my life if I could only clarify in what ways I needed help. But inside I still struggled with a deeper issue; although I was wanting help, was I really worth the time and attention of a mentor? It was there I needed to take a risk and step beyond my insecurity. I asked a leader who was well respected in the area of my needs to mentor me through a real need that I had. To my utter amazement he said yes.

Mentoring and You

These two stories come from the journeys of people just like you. Parts of their stories may be similar to yours. Whether you have had mentors, or struggle to find mentors, this workbook can help you find mentors.

Mentoring

"Mentoring is a relational experience in which one person empowers another by sharing God-given resources" (*Connecting*, Paul Stanley and J. Robert Clinton, p. 33).

Mentoring is making the mentor's personal strengths, resources, and networks (friendships/contacts) available to help a protege (mentoree) reach his or her goals.

The **mentor** is the person who shares the God-given resources.

The **mentoree** is the person being empowered. The transfer between the mentor and mentoree is called **empowerment.**

The resources which are shared in a mentoring relationship could include:

- wisdom and discernment
- life and ministry experience
- timely advice
- new methods
- skills
- principles
- important values and lessons
- organizational influence
- financial resources

The Typical Pathway to Mentoring

There are five dynamics on the path to a mentoring relationships. These dynamics define five aspects of mentoring.

1. **Attraction**—Like attracts like. People naturally move towards those who seem helpful. Mentorees may be attracted by a mentor's personality, spirituality, ministry skills, or experience.
2. **Relationship**—The best exchanges of empowerment resources happen when mentors and mentorees trust each other.
3. **Responsiveness**—The mentoree's willingness to respond to the mentor's information is vital for learning empowerment.
4. **Accountability**—Mentorees must answer to someone for their growth and spiritual development. Often there is mutual accountability between mentors and mentorees.
5. **Empowerment**—This is the actual exchange of resources and encouragement between mentor and mentoree in areas of life and ministry.

The Typical Mentoring Relationship

A mentoree usually seeks the help of a mentor in a needed area of resourcing and takes the first step in the relationship.

A good mentoring relationship happens naturally, with little discussion of the type of mentoring. Realistically, both mentor and the mentoree are often uncertain about the relationship and need help in defining it. They need to clarify their roles and agree on the necessary type and kind of mentoring the mentoree seeks.

What can mentorees do to help mentoring occur?

Successful mentoring hinges on the <u>relationship</u> between the mentor and mentoree. One essential characteristic of the relationship, from the mentorees point of view, is the issue of <u>submission</u>. At the heart of a submissive relationship lies respect for the mentor, appreciation for qualities seen, desires to be like the mentor or to be able to do what the mentor can do.

Mentorees can also help to contribute in other ways:

1. Accept responsibility for growth—We each stand accountable to God for the stewardship of our gifts, abilities, personal growth, and development. The initiative rests with the mentoree, not with someone else.

2. Develop a personal understanding of God's direction—Mentorees need a general understanding of how God has shaped them—through gifts, calling, strengths and weaknesses—to pinpoint their mentoring needs.

3. Develop personal and ministry goals—Self-aware mentorees set goals for personal and ministry formation. Lateral or peer mentors can help mentorees set specific, attainable goals.

4. Match mentors with goals—Once goals have been identified, mentorees should pray and seek for mentors who could help them meet their goals.

5. Develop mentoring eyes—God is sovereignly at work in each mentoree's development. "Mentoring eyes" means recognizing divine appointments and growth opportunities that God puts in a mentoree's path.

6. Maintain a teachable spirit—Little can occur in the mentoring relationship unless the mentoree has a hunger to learn, listen, and respond positively to input from the mentor.

7. Continue to trust God for development—Mentoring is enhanced as mentorees continue to affirm their trust in God and His timing in their life and development. Trusting God means not getting frustrated when doors have not opened in expected ways, or that resources are not present to meet the challenges.

Influencers in the Past

Mentoring has often occurred unaware.
List individuals in your past that have helped you in your growth and development.

Who has provided you with: wisdom and discernment
life and ministry experience
timely advice
new methods
new skills
key principles or insights
important values and lessons
organizational influence
financial resources

List those individuals who have most influenced you and your walk with Christ.		
Date	Name	How They Influenced You

Mentoring Check

1. Did your list include family, siblings, spouses?
2. Did your list include Biblical characters that you have studied, and who have influenced you?
3. Did your list include biographies of lives that have influenced you through your reading?
4. Did your list include contemporary believers and leaders you admire, but not met?

The Point: There have been more mentors in your past than you have acknowledged.

Mentoring
Assessing Your Needs

STEP 2

Identifying Mentors

- Mentoring is relational empowerment.
- Mentors share resources; mentorees receive empowerment.
- Mentors provide encouragement, support, and the link to resources, often through the modelling of ministry.
- Mentorees facilitate their own empowerment by taking responsibility for their own growth and remaining teachable.
- There are at least nine different types of mentors.
- Mentors can provide intensive, occasional, or passive mentoring.

- One key to mentoring is understanding the different types of mentors and the mentoring help you need.

You will need ... Workbook and pen

Time required ... Approximately 1 hour

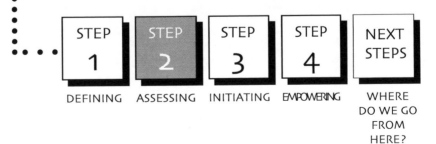

STEP 1	STEP 2	STEP 3	STEP 4	NEXT STEPS
DEFINING	ASSESSING	INITIATING	EMPOWERING	WHERE DO WE GO FROM HERE?

Assessing Nine Types of Mentors

STEP 2

One way to identify future mentors is to expand your definition of mentors. Listed below are nine different types of mentors—and their major thrusts—that could help with your development as a believer.

1. **Discipler**—A discipler is a more experienced follower who imparts to a new believer the knowledge, skills and basics to grow in Christ. Disciplers affect the new believer's character and behavior.

2. **Spiritual Guide**—A spiritual guide mentor is a mature follower of Christ who shares knowledge and skills related to greater spirituality. Spiritual guides offer accountability and insights for the mentoree's spiritual growth.

3. **Coach**—This mentor knows how to do something well and how to communicate the skill.

4. **Counselor**—This mentor provides counsel and advice at crucial times, such as decision making and transition.

5. **Teacher**—The teacher provides knowledge and the ability to communicate that knowledge. Teachers offer perspective and enhancement to ministry.

6. **Sponsor**—The sponsor has credibility, positional, or spiritual authority within an organization, which enables a mentoree to develop and advance within that organization. Mentors often provide influence and protection.

7. **Contemporary Model**—This is an exemplary person who indirectly imparts skills, lessons for life, ministry, and values.

8. **Historical Model**—This is a person from the past who serves as a model through books, biographies, and autobiographies. Empowerment comes through example, ministry lessons, and life values.

9. **Divine Contact**—The divine contact is a mentor whom God brings into contact with a person at a critical, unplanned moment in order to bring new insight or discernment.

    -   Identifying mentor types helps to address the problem of a lack of mentors.
    -   Instead of holding to the concept that there is one mentor who must provide all the empowerment, the preceding list shows that there could be several mentors who could fulfill an individual's mentoring needs.

Paul and Barnabas

Barnabas serves as a major mentoring example in the Scriptures. As many have noted, Barnabas never wrote Scripture like Paul or Luke, but neither could have made their impact without Barnabas.

In Acts 9:27 Barnabas championed Paul's cause with the Apostles at Jerusalem. A mentor has the insight to see <u>potential</u> in a leader although the person may have a bad reputation or abrasive personality traits. Often strong leadership qualities are hidden beneath confrontive, abrasive, and impatient personalities. A mentor is often willing to take a risk and sponsor a potential leader. Barnabas did so for Paul.

A mentor is willing to co-minister with a potential leader in order to raise the experience and status levels of the leader. Barnabas went to Tarsus in Acts 11:25 and persuaded Paul to come and minister with him. He was mentoring. This single act by Barnabas was a major link in the bridging of the Gospel to the Gentile world. Where would we be without Barnabas? Many lessons on mentoring flow from Barnabas' ministry.

Note: Barnabas and Paul went through changes in their mentoring relationship: from an intensive period of coaching, to a time of sponsoring Paul into the early church, to a time of Barnabas becoming more of a periodic, divine contact for Paul.
Also note that their relationship moves into a more co-mentoring relationship as it evolved.
Mentoring intensity can be viewed as a continuum, utilizing the nine types of mentors (see below).

Mentors can help believers
- learn the basics of walking with Christ (disciplers)
- learn how to mature in depth in their Christian life (spirituality mentors)
- learn to do things (coaches)
- learn by giving wise advice to help them through situations (counselors)
- learn necessary ideas and get perspectives (teachers)

Mentoring Continuum

The nine types of mentors can be put into three categories according to mentoring relationship intensity.

Intensive	Occasional	Passive
1. Discipler	4. Counselor	7. Contemp. Model
2. Spiritual Guide	5. Teacher	8. Historical Model
3. Coach	6. Sponsor	9. Divine Contact

More Deliberate --- > Less Deliberate

STEP 1

Review the results of the **"Influencers in My Past"** exercise found on p. 12. For each of the influencers that you identified, go back and evaluate which of nine types they might have been.

Note: Often certain types reccur. This may give you insight into how God seeks to influence your development.

STEP 2 Before we can find personal mentors, we must first determine mentoring needs. Below, list prioritized goals for your life and ministry for the next 12-18 months.

| Life Development Goals (BEING) | Ministry Development Goals (DOING) |

Life Development Goals
(BEING)

My current growth goals for my personal growth would be to ...

1. _____

2. _____

3. _____

Based upon your life goals, what help do you need to accomplish the above goals?

MENTORING NEEDS

1. _____

2. _____

3. _____

Based upon your mentoring needs, which of the nine mentors will you need to address the above need?

TYPE OF MENTORS

1. _____

2. _____

3. _____

Ministry Development Goals
(DOING)

My current growth goals for my ministry-work is to ...

1. _____

2. _____

3. _____

Based upon your ministry goals, what help do you need to accomplish the above goals?

MENTORING NEEDS

1. _____

2. _____

3. _____

Based upon your mentoring needs, which of the nine mentors will you need to address the above need?

TYPE OF MENTORS

1. _____

2. _____

3. _____

Discipler
Spiritual Guide
Coach
Counselor
Teacher
Sponsor
Contemporary Model
Historical Model
Divine Contact

Initiating
The Mentoring
Relationship

Launching the Mentoring Relationship

The nine types of mentors and three categories (intense-occasional-passive) mentors help to view mentoring with a new set of eyes and recognize the potential of mentors.

It is quite possible that God has already placed in your path the mentors you need.

Once identified, the mentoring relationships you need must be initiated.

In this next step, you will be developing a mentoring constellation and learn how you can initiate new mentoring relationships.

You will need ... Work completed in steps one and two

Time required ... Approximately 2-3 hours

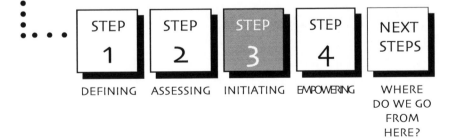

STEP 1	STEP 2	STEP 3	STEP 4	NEXT STEPS
DEFINING	ASSESSING	INITIATING	EMPOWERING	WHERE DO WE GO FROM HERE?

Three Kinds of Mentoring

STEP 3

"Christian workers need relationships that will mentor us, peers who will co-mentor us, and people that we are mentoring. This will help ensure a balanced and healthy perspective on life and ministry," says J. Robert Clinton in *Please Mentor Me* (p. 27).

Lifelong development is greatly enhanced by a balance of mentoring relationships. There are three basic kinds of mentoring: upward mentoring, co-mentoring (internal and external), and downward mentoring.

Upward Mentoring—Upward mentoring pushes people forward to expand their potential. Upward mentors see the bigger picture and how the current situation fits into that picture. Their experience and knowledge base is more advanced than the mentoree. They give valuable advice and challenge the mentoree to persevere and grow.

Co-Mentoring—Co-mentoring is lateral mentoring that comes from peers who are either inside or outside a person's daily frame of reference.

Internal co-mentors are peers in the same ministry environment and about the same level of spiritual maturity. They provide mutual growth and accountability, contextual insights within the organizations, and friendship during difficulty.

External co-mentors are peers like internal co-mentors, except they are outside the ministry situation. They are also at about the same level of development and maturity. They provide objective perspective. They challenge a person to think through the way they act and apply insights.

Downward Mentoring—Believers need to identify, select, and help develop emerging disciples. Downward mentoring means empowering younger or less experienced individuals. Downward mentors provide accountability, challenge, insight, and critical skills. Downward mentoring also counter-balances the tendency for disciples to plateau and become inconsistent in living out their values.

The Mentoring Constellation

The three kinds of mentoring are displayed in the following model developed by Dr. Robert J. Clinton and Dr. Paul Stanley.

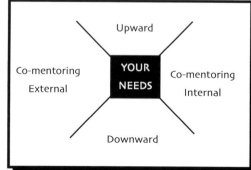

Sample Constellation

Upward Mentors
(those ahead of me)
1. Bobby Clinton / Teacher
2. Barnabas / Hist. Model

Lateral Mentors
(external)
1. Matt / Coach
2. Rick / Contemp. Model

Mentoring Needs

1. Leading an Org.
2. Intimacy w/ Christ
3. Leader development
4. Ministry Expansion

Lateral Mentors
(internal)
1. Sam / Coach
2. Tom / Spiritual Guide

Downward Mentors
(those I can mentor)
1. Brad / Coach
2. Rick / Coach-Teacher
3. Gary / Sponsor- Counselor
4. Buck / Sponsor-Coach

STEP 1

Review the Mentoring Constellation above.
Note: Not all mentors are active at the same time.
Note: Lateral mentoring is less formal; upward-downward more structured

<u>**EXERCISE:**</u>   Place your top mentoring needs (p. 16) in the middle box below.
List names and type of mentor in the four quadrants.

My Mentoring Constellation

Upward Mentors
(those ahead of me)

Lateral Mentors
(external)

Mentoring Needs

1.
2.
3.
4.

Lateral Mentors
(internal)

Downward Mentors
(those I can mentor)

Initiating the Relationship

The Typical Pathway to Mentoring

Review again the five parts of a mentoring relationship.
These dynamics can help you to clarify potential mentors.

1. **Attraction**—Like attracts like. People naturally move towards those who seem helpful. Mentorees may be attracted by a mentor's personality, spirituality, ministry skills, or experience.
2. **Relationship**—The best exchanges of empowerment resources happen when mentors and mentorees trust each other.
3. **Responsiveness**—The mentoree's willingness to respond to the mentor's information is vital for learning empowerment.
4. **Accountability**—Mentorees must answer to someone for their growth and spiritual development. Often there is mutual accountability between mentors and mentorees.
5. **Empowerment**—This is the actual exchange of resources and encouragement between mentor and mentoree in areas of life and ministry.

Where to Begin?

1. If you don't know who first to ask, start with the top three candidates related to your top needs. Mentorees are often surprised at how willing mentors are to help.
2. Approach the mentor with your mentoring goals and the ways you feel he or she might be able to help. Allow the mentor to give input and help clarify your issues and define your goals.
3. Ask for a first meeting to discuss the issues. After meeting together, you and the mentor will have a much better idea whether the relationship is something you want to pursue. Determine the type and length of mentoring.

Clarifying the Mentoring Relationships

1. Show your current mentor the definitions in *Mentoring,* especially the types of mentors and the kinds of mentoring. Discuss your past mentoring in light of these definitions. Review ways you might want to adjust the relationship in order to become more focused or intentional.
2. Be careful not to put the relationship under undue pressure. If it has been an effective mentoring relationship to date, then do not sacrifice the friendship by formal structure.
3. Set up clear relationship guidelines when appropriate, such as the nature of accountability, lines of communication, issues of confidentiality, length of time for the relationship, and time for re-evaluation.
4. Bring closure to the relationship when the mentoring exchange is complete.

The Ten Commandments of a Mentoring Relationship
Guidelines for the Mentoring Relationship

The "Ten Commandments" of mentoring, developed by Dr. J. Robert Clinton and Dr. Paul Stanley in their book *Connecting*, help guide mentoring relationships to greater effectiveness. Use these as a general guide, but do not let the relational aspects be hampered by unnecessary formality.

1. Establish the relationship. Sometimes mentoring relationships just happen. Sometimes they are developed and cultivated. Mentoring has a better chance for empowerment when a relationship is clearly established.

2. Jointly agree on the purpose of the mentoring relationship. By spelling out the expectations, you can avoid unfulfilled expectations and disappointments.

3. Determine how often you will meet.

4. Determine the nature of accountability. Agree together on how the accountability will be set up and monitored. It can happen through written reports, phone calls, or general verbal feedback.

5. Set up clear lines of communication. Discuss when, how often, and by what means you will interact. Also discuss the freedom on behalf of mentor and mentoree in questioning and discussing topics.

6. Clarify confidentiality.

7. Agree upon the length of time. Time limits keep the relationship fresh and give opportunity for review and evaluation.

8. From time to time, evaluate the process and mentoring effectiveness. This will help ensure that the relationship is meeting the needs of the mentoree and is not burdensome for the mentor.

9. Continually match expectations to fit the current mentoring situation. Maintain flexibility and adaptability.

10. Bring closure to the mentoring relationship. Mentoring should "begin with the end in mind." Both should agree that mentoring is completed. If done right, closure can increase the level of accomplishment.

STEP 2

Without an intentional plan, your mentoring will most likely fall into the "important, but not urgent" basket! You need a plan!

<u>EXERCISE:</u> Using your Mentoring Constellation (p. 19), write out your action steps for the next 60-days to secure mentors for your development.

	Potential Mentor	Mentoring Need	Type	Contact Date
1.				
2.				
3.				
4.				

Accountability

What question do you need to be ask in the next 30/60 days to help ensure you are working on finding mentors? Who will ask you that question?

_____

Mentoring
Summary: Core Concepts

- Mentoring is relational empowerment.
- Mentors share resources; mentorees receive empowerment.
- Mentors provide encouragement, support, and the link to resources, often through the modelling of ministry.
- Mentorees facilitate their own empowerment by taking responsibility for growing and remaining teachable.
- There are at least nine different types of mentors.
- Mentors can provide intensive, occasional, or passive mentoring.
- Clarifying goals and mentoring helps to identify the type of mentoring needed.
- Mentoring constellation portrays the mentoring needs.
- The mentoring Ten Commandments guide the development of a mentoring relationship.
- Without an action plan, your mentoring may not occur.

Mentoring
Helping Others Find Mentors

STEP 4

Effective servants recognize mentoring as a priority.

They are committed to being mentored and mentoring others.

They recognize that helping others ultimately causes great growth in his or her own life.

- You are a potential mentor
- You can help others find mentors
- Most people feel incapable or ill-equipped to mentor
- Most people do not know where to start

This final step is designed to help you consider becoming a mentor by introducing you to three resources:

- Resources to clarify your role as a mentor; either peer or downward mentoring
- Resources to help a small or large group become exposed to mentoring
- Resources to help an individual find personal mentors

You will need ... completed Mentoring Constellation

Time required ... Approximately 1 hour to review materials

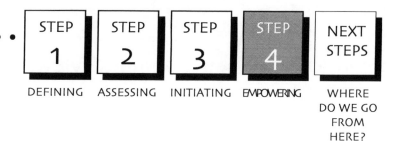

STEP 1	STEP 2	STEP 3	STEP 4	NEXT STEPS
DEFINING	ASSESSING	INITIATING	EMPOWERING	WHERE DO WE GO FROM HERE?

Helping Others Find Mentors

STEP 4

Steps in Mentoring Others

1. Clarify the personal goals and resourcing needs of those you desire to help. Have him or her reflect on current situation and vision for the future?
2. List the desired resources needed to address mentoring needs. Help him or her recognize additional needs. Arrive together at essential needs.
3. Discuss together the prioritizing of these needs. Explore the type and kinds of mentoring needed: upward mentors help mentorees acquire skills and knowledge, co-mentors clarify and apply insights to the particular situation.
4. Create a list of potential mentors and construct a mentoring constellation of existing and potential mentors. Encourage pursuing new mentoring relationships, even those not normally accessible. If these potential mentors cannot participate, they can often link the mentoree to other candidates.
5. Challenge the believer to identify two or three servants to whom he or she could offer a mentoring relationship. Each of us needs to be empowering new leaders through sharing his God-given resources.

Are You Willing?

1. Be open and willing to help others, by sharing your resources.
2. Do not put yourself under the pressure that you must assume responsibility for another person's effectiveness. Instead, just be ready to play a small part in their ongoing contribution for God's Kingdom.
3. Review the resources on p. 25-26 to help you determine what resources you could offer someone else.

Introducing Mentoring / Group Exercise

Before individuals can find mentors, they first may need to be introduced to the paradigm of mentoring. Review the resources on pp. 27-29 for introducing mentoring to a small or large group.

Conducting a Mentoring Interview

You may or may not be the mentor an individual needs. The Interview Guide on pp. 30-32 provides step-by-step for you to assist someone in determining the mentors he or she may need.

You and Mentoring
Obstacles to Becoming a Mentor

There are four common objections that often hold potential mentors back from mentoring others.

1. **"I can't mentor someone else, I am not there yet myself!**
   Like attracts like. People are drawn to those who they feel might be helpful. They are not looking for an expert. They are looking for someone who is on a similar journey.
2. **"There are so many people that would be better than myself!"**
   There is always someone more qualified. The point is not whether you are fully qualified, but what you have learned along the way might help someone else be more effective.
3. **"I am not equipped to be a mentor!"**
   Mentoring is a relationship. By reviewing the concepts of this workbook, you now have the framework. Make yourself available. You will be amazed at how God will use you.
4. **"What if the mentoring I offer is not what they really needed?"**
   Mentoring relationships can always be re-negotiated. All relationships should be re-evaluated. You may be the one that helps network them to needed resources.

What type of mentoring help can you offer?

1. Brainstorm resources and experience areas in which you could use to make a contribution to others:

   _____
   _____
   _____
   _____

> **Potential Mentoring Areas:**
> wisdom and discernment
> life and ministry experience
> timely advice
> new methods
> new skills
> key principles or insights
> important values and lessons
> organizational influence
> financial resources
> others

2. Review the nine mentor types. FIRST, check the type you have done in the past, and SECOND check the type you would like (or desire) to do in the future.

Nine Mentor Types	Done in Past	Desire for future
Discipler	_____	_____
Spiritual Guide	_____	_____
Coach	_____	_____
Counselor	_____	_____
Teacher	_____	_____
Sponsor	_____	_____
Contemporary Model	_____	_____
Historical Model	_____	_____
Divine Contact	_____	_____

Clarifying Your Mentoring Five Circles

If you are involved in leadership, there is often more people who need mentoring than you can mentor. Examining the life of Christ reveals he experienced a smiliar dilema. If you evaluate how Jesus ministered, you begin to see that He operates on different levels of relationship and mentoring. He was able to focus on the few, yet offer help to the many. Notice the five circles of mentoring below.

As the circles moved inward, Jesus offer greater insights and a greater investment of time.

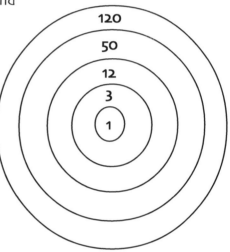

120 =	Wider audience	Less deliberate
50=	Followers	
12=	Disciples	
3=	Peter,James and John	
1=	Peter	More deliberate

Note: Your numbers will be different, but each level is distinguished by two criteria:
1. Amount of time invested
2. Amount of input given

The closer toward the center, the greater the time-input

Your Mentoring

Who?

Who would you place in the five levels?

Level 5:

Level 4:

Level 3:

Level 2:

Level 1:

What?

What resourcing can or will you offer people in the five levels?

Level 5:

Level 4:

Level 3:

Level 2:

Level 1:

Two-Hour Exercise
Notes for Introducing Mentoring

Principle: Effective believers and servants maintain a learning posture throughout life. They have had a series of meaningful relationships (mentors) that have enhanced their development.

Definition of mentoring: "A relational experience in which one person empowers another by sharing God-given resources." —Paul Stanley and J. Robert Clinton, *Connecting*

Exercise: (1) Open the exercise by asking the participants to list those who have most influenced their lives and ministries. (2) Next, ask them to record the impact of their influence (i.e., about relationships, leading a group, etc.). For now, leave the kind and the type blank.
(3) Once complete, ask the participants to reflect on the following questions: How many listed a leader from church history? How many listed a biblical leader? How many listed their spouse? How many listed current contemporary leaders. The point: To change how we view mentoring and recognize there are more mentors available than we may have first thought.

Review the nine types of mentors in three categories. Give personal examples where appropriate. Refer back to the first exercise and attempt to identify the type.

Next, further expand their views of mentoring by discussing the three kinds of mentors: upward, lateral and downward. Upward and downward are often more formal. Lateral is often informal. Again, return to the first exercise and try to clarify the kind of mentoring.

Finding Mentors

The process presented is a guide for obtaining mentors. There are always exceptions. The steps presented assist in becoming more intentional.

1. Summarize your personal calling. (What has God called a leader to do?)
2. List your personal and ministry growth goals for the next 12 months.
3. Prioritize your mentoring needs. (Pinpointing of needs helps unlock a mentor's contribution.)
4. Identify the types and kinds of mentors the mentoree could be seeking.
5. Brainstorm possible candidates. (Don't forget contemporary and historical models.) Seek the advice and input from leaders you respect.
6. Contact potential mentors. Ask for an initial meeting and a trial relationship. Encourage the participants to seek the best possible candidates. They might say yes.

Closure: Challenge the participants to thank their past mentors and to begin now to pray not only for their own future mentors but also concerning whom God would allow them to mentor.

Introducing Mentoring

Effective believers and servants maintain a learning posture throughout life. They have had a series of meaningful relationships (mentors) that have enhanced their development. Once vision becomes clear, the issue then becomes obtaining the resources that will be necessary to accomplish your vision. *"Mentoring is a relational experience in which one person empowers another by sharing God-given resources."*

— Paul Stanley and J. Robert Clinton, *Connecting*

Exercise: Influencers in My Past

o List those individuals who have most influenced you and your ministry. List leaders, friends, authors, etc. (Fill in everything except the type and the kind.)

Date	Name	How They Influenced You	Type

The Point: There are more mentors available than you may have first thought.

Nine Types and Three Kinds

Understanding the types and kinds helps you to better recognize potential mentors.

Mentoring Type	Mentoring Help
1. Discipler	Enables in the basics of the faith
2. Spiritual Guide	Gives accountability for personal and spiritual growth
3. Coach	Facilitates greater skill and motivational enablement
4. Counselor	Gives perspective, timely advice on self and ministry
5. Teacher	Imparts knowledge, wisdom and conceptual insights
6. Sponsor	Provides career guidance and organizational help
7. Contemporary Model	Serves as a model and example for life and ministry
8. Historical Model	Highlights principles and values from the past for life and ministry
9. Divine Contact	Provides timely guidance and discernment

Three Kinds of Mentoring

Christian leaders need relationships that will enhance their growth and development:

- Mentors who are ahead of a leader's development
- Peer co-mentors
- Those whom a leader is seeking to help

These three kinds of mentoring help ensure a balanced and healthy perspective to life and ministry.

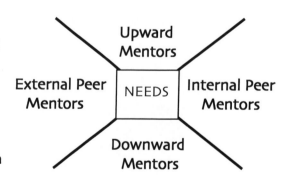

Reflection

o Go back to the earlier exercise ("Mentors in Your Past") and try to identify the type of mentor each of your past influencers may have been. They could have been more than one type. Then determine whether it is upward or peer mentoring.

Helping Others
Find Mentors

Six Practical Steps for Coaching Someone to Find Mentors

o Summarize his or her personal calling.
o List personal and ministry growth goals for the next 12 - 18 months.
o Prioritize mentoring needs. Be specific in defining his or her actual need and how you believe a mentor could assist you.

o Identify the types of mentors that might be needed.
o Brainstorm possible candidates. (Don't forget contemporary and historical models.) Encourage them to seek advice and input from additional leaders.
o Set-up a plan to contact potential mentors, detailing mentoring needs and their role, using one of the types. Their task: Ask for an initial meeting to explain their needs and potentially begin a trial relationship.

Accountability

It may be helpful for the individual to have a deadline for obtaining mentors. If so, set up an additional time together to review the leader's progress within 30-60 days.

If YOU are entering the mentoring relationship with this individual...
Three Tips for your Mentoring Relationship

1. Jointly agree on the purpose of the mentoring relationship.
2. Determine the nature of accountability and confidentiality.
3. Commit to evaluate from time to time. Bring closure when mentoring goals have been accomplished, or when either part desires to end the formal mentoring relationship.

Interview Guide Work sheets

On pp. 31-32, the work sheets help to walk you through a one-to-one mentoring interview.
- Use these notes as a guide for your discussion with an individual
- Give the work sheets to the individual when completed.
- Make additional copies of work sheets to work with other individuals.

Other Resources:
Paul Stanley and J. Robert Clinton, *Connecting,* NavPress
Robert Biehl, *Mentoring,* Masterplanning Group
Ted Engstrom, *The Fine Art of Mentoring*

1. Present Goals / Personal Vision

My current growth goal for my personal life would be to ...

My current growth goal for my ministry-work life is to ...

I have a personal vision to see ...

2. Mentoring Needs / Personal Growth

I feel God is calling me to grow in the area of ...

I feel the greatest challenge I am facing in ministry would be ...

My greatest need for mentoring would be ...

3. From the responses in question 1 and 2, prioritize your mentoring goals and needs. Be specific by defining the actual need.

GOAL   NEED (Help required by Mentor)

1.
2.
3.
4.

4. Potential Mentors for You

If you could ask any mentor to help you address your mentoring needs, who would you ask first? Who would you ask next? Who else would you ask? Who from history could you study? What biblical leader might you study?

1.
2.
3.
4.

Mentoring Constellation

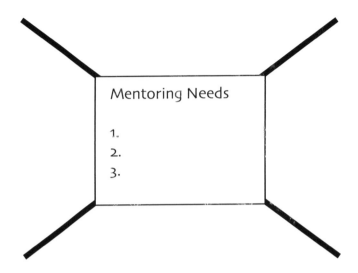

Mentoring Needs

1.
2.
3.

5. Your Mentoring of Others (Downward)
List three individuals that you feel you could offer some help or share some of your resources in order to increase their effectiveness as a child of God.

1.
2.
3.

6. Mentoring ACTION Plan

Potential Mentor	Mentoring Need	Contact Date	Response
1.			
2.			
3.			
4.			

7. Accountability
Do we need to meet again to check on your progress? **Yes or No?**
If yes, date: _____

Mentoring
The Next Step

Where do we go from here?

Mentoring concludes the personal development process called *Focused Living.* The process moves an individual toward living a more focused life that pleases God, and finishes well.

The *Focused Living* process involved three-steps:

- *Perspective* helps believers assess their past

- *Focus* helps believers clarify their future through the development of a Personal Calling statement.

- *Mentoring* helps believers to assess their resources for accomplishing their personal calling.

- The next step is deciding how to use the *Focused Living* process in your church is on the next page. **Turn to p. 34.**

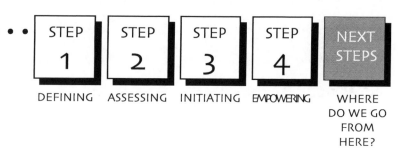

STEP 1	STEP 2	STEP 3	STEP 4	NEXT STEPS
DEFINING	ASSESSING	INITIATING	EMPOWERING	WHERE DO WE GO FROM HERE?

MOVE YOUR INTENT INTO NEW BEHAVIOR!

The 100-Day Plan

APEX focused on helping you clarify your contribution.

What happens next will help to determine if the time you invested in the APEX process will make any difference. What you do during your first 100 days by way of coaching and accountability will help to ensure long-term implementation.

The first 100 days after any breakthrough experience is key to securing the change and translating that experience into new long-term behavior for any leader.

Holistic Change... applying your results to each of the FOUR spheres of Influence:

Family: Arena of influence that includes parents, spouse, children, extended family, and friends.
Vocation: Arena of influence including your place of work, profession, career, and/or job opportunities.
Community: Arena of influence including your local neighborhood, city, county, or society at large.
Church   Arena of influence that starts with your local church body and moves to the wider world.

The 100-Day Plan is an intentional implementation tool designed to help you secure the change that has occurred as a result of the APEX breakthrough experience.

The 100-Day Plan is a challenge to intentionally script the next 100 Days so you create short-term wins that reflect the gain you achieved from your Breakthru experience.

THE BEST PART IS THAT THE 100-DAY PLAN is a FREE RESOURCE.
DOWNLOAD THE FREE COACHING RESOURCES AND AUDIO PODCAST
at the Leader Breakthru website.

**GO TO THE LEADER BREAKTHRU UNIVERSITY HOME PAGE AND CLICK
THE RESOURCES BUTTON**
OR, go to http://www.leaderbreakthru.com/resources/free-resources.php

THERE IS NO BETTER TIME THAN NOW TO GET STARTED!

www.leaderbreakthru.com

Focused LIVING

Clarifying Calling

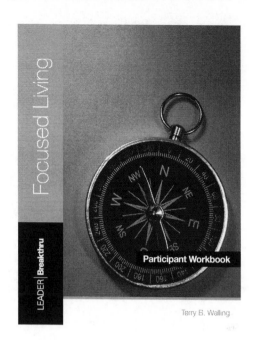

Focused Living

Participant Workbook

LEADER | Breakthru

Terry B. Walling

What is Focused Living?

Focused Living is a personal development discovery process that helps leaders clarify their life direction and personal calling.

Each of us is being shaped by God to make a unique and ultimate contribution (Ephesians 2:10).

The question is not whether God is at work, but knowing how to better recognize (1) what God is at work doing, and (2) how to set a course-direction to align with His work.

Over 20,000 leaders have experienced the Focused Living process in more than ten languages. It seeks to address three core questions:

Where have you been?

Where are you going?

Who can help you get there?

What are the take-aways?

1. Personal Timeline
2. Statement of Personal Calling
3. 100-Day Plan and link to Mentoring

Topic:	Calling and issues of Identity and Direction
Who:	For leaders seeking greater focus and clarity; can apply to leaders as early as 20s-30s.
What:	Focused Living Retreat, Focused Living Small Group, and Focused Living On-LINE
Time:	FL Retreat (8-Sessions of 1.5 hours) FL SMALL Group (10 Sessions) FL On-LINE (12–15 hours)
Resources:	Focused Living Workbook Focused Living On-LINE process Focused Living Small Group Resource
Online:	www.leaderbreakthru.com/training/focused-living-online/
Exercises:	**Personal Timeline,** First Order of Calling (being), Core Values, Second Order of Calling (doing), Surrender, The 100-Day Plan
More Info:	www.leaderbreakthru.com

Every Leader Needs...

SOVEREIGN *Perspective*

Transitions	**Focused Living**	**APEX**	**Resonance**
Awakening (CALLING)	**CALLING**	**CONTRIBUTION**	**CONVERGENCE**
Deciding (CONTRIBUTION)	Clarity of	Discovery of	Choosing to
Finishing (CONVERGENCE)	Direction	Unique ROLE	Finish Well

SITUATIONAL *Coaching*

Bite-Sized ONLINE video modules and worksheets delivered just-in-time to meet the immediate needs that all leaders face.

Through **Leader Breakthru University** leaders get the help, when they need the help, in the trenches as they face the challenges.

Made in the USA
San Bernardino, CA
24 June 2016